QUIZ
GAMES
FOR
BRIGHT
SPARKS

Puzzles and solutions by
Dr Gareth Moore
B.Sc (Hons) M.Phil Ph.D

Illustrations by Jess Bradley

Designed by Zoe Bradley
Edited by Sue McMillan and Katy Lennon
Cover design by John Bigwood

QUIZ GAMES

FOR

BRIGHT SPARKS

Buster Books

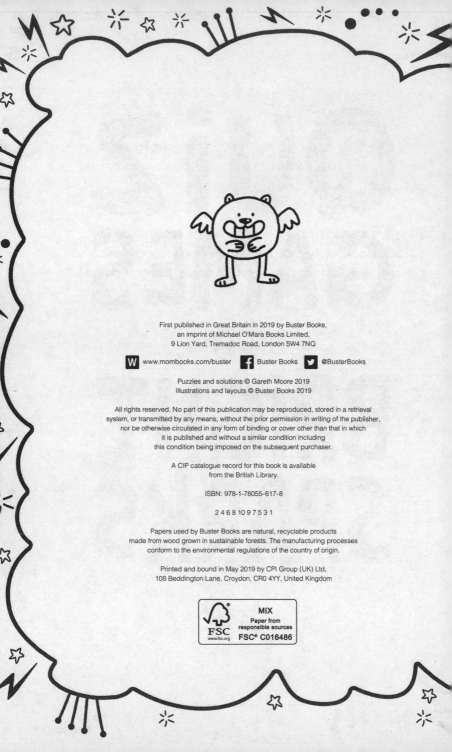

First published in Great Britain in 2019 by Buster Books,
an imprint of Michael O'Mara Books Limited,
9 Lion Yard, Tremadoc Road, London SW4 7NQ

W www.mombooks.com/buster f Buster Books 🐦 @BusterBooks

Puzzles and solutions © Gareth Moore 2019
Illustrations and layouts © Buster Books 2019

A CIP catalogue record for this book is available
from the British Library.

ISBN: 978-1-78055-617-8

2 4 6 8 10 9 7 5 3 1

Papers used by Buster Books are natural, recyclable products
made from wood grown in sustainable forests. The manufacturing processes
conform to the environmental regulations of the country of origin.

Printed and bound in May 2019 by CPI Group (UK) Ltd,
108 Beddington Lane, Croydon, CR0 4YY, United Kingdom

MIX
Paper from
responsible sources
FSC® C016486
FSC
www.fsc.org

INTRODUCTION

Are you feeling quizzical? Then kick-start your brain for some mind-boggling quiz questions that will test your knowledge and teach you some amazing facts along the way.

There are two main types of quiz in the book: quick-fire quizzes and word jumbles. The quick-fire quizzes are great to test yourself with and, once you're a quiz pro, you can use them to test your friends and family. For the word jumbles, you'll need to draw lines to match either the pairs or the sets of three answers. Do this in pencil in case you make a mistake — you don't want to get in a tangle.

There's space on the pages to make notes as you go, but if you need more room to work out your answers, you can use the note pages at the back of the book.

If you find any of the questions too difficult and you don't know the answer, don't panic! You might still be able to work it out. Stop and think about the subject, is there anything you do know about it? If you still struggle, then make a guess or ask someone else. As a last resort, all the answers are at the back of the book. Either way, you'll learn something new!

Use the score box at the bottom of each page to note down how many answers you got right. Once you've completed all the quizzes you will be a trivia champion!

Good luck, and have fun!

Introducing the Quiz Master:
Gareth Moore, B.Sc (Hons) M.Phil Ph.D

Dr Gareth Moore is an Ace Puzzler, and author of many puzzle and brain-training books.

He created an online brain-training site, BrainedUp.com, and runs the online puzzle site PuzzleMix.com. Gareth has a Ph.D from the University of Cambridge, where he taught machines to understand spoken English.

PLANT OR ANIMAL?

The names of five animals and five plants have been muddled together, and it's your job to sort them out into their two sets. To sort them, draw a leaf in the box if you think it's a plant, or an animal if you think it's an animal.

 plant

 animal

carrot ☐   holly ☐

dandelion ☐   horse ☐

dolphin ☐   lion ☐

fern ☐   kangaroo ☐

garlic ☐   zebra ☐

SCORE

....

Circle the correct answer for each question.

1. On which part of your body would you wear a baseball cap?

a. hands   b. feet

c. around your shoulders   d. head

2. Which of these accessories isn't usually made of metal?

a. scarf   b. bracelet

c. necklace   d. earring

3. Which of these is not usually worn in a pair?

a. slipper   b. sneaker   c. sock   d. sweater

4. Which of these metals would be the most expensive option for a bracelet?

a. platinum   b. gold   c. silver   d. copper

5. Where would you normally wear a wedding ring?

a. ring finger on left hand

b. ring finger on right hand

c. little finger on left hand

d. little finger on right hand

SCORE

....

1. Every snowflake is made up of tiny crystals of which of the following?

a. snow
c. ice
b. rain
d. dust

2. Which of the following words is used to describe snow that melts as it falls from the sky?

a. hail b. rain c. fog d. sleet

3. Which of the following items is most associated with cold weather?

a. gloves b. shorts c. swimsuit d. sandals

4. What can be formed by water that freezes as it drips?

a. igloo b. ice cube c. icicle d. snowman

5. Which of the following winter sports has events that include cross-country, slalom and jumping?

a. skiing
c. curling
b. ice hockey
d. snowboarding

SCORE

....

Each of these nine things is usually a shade of white, orange or pink. There are three whites, three oranges and three pinks. Can you match them correctly? The first one has been done for you.

carrot

cream   white

flamingo

pearl

piglet   orange

pumpkin

raspberry

snow   pink

tangerine

SCORE

UNDERWATER WORLD

1. Which of the following sea creatures is a mammal, not a fish?

   a. shark   b. tuna   c. clownfish   d. dolphin

2. Which of these animals can spray ink into the water?

   a. eel   b. starfish   c. octopus   d. pufferfish

3. Which underwater animal makes the loudest noises?

   a. dolphin   b. sperm whale
   c. stingray   d. sea urchin

4. Which of these animals makes a pearl within its shell?

   a. oyster   b. crab
   c. turtle   d. snail

5. Which of these animals is also known as a 'killer whale'?

   a. orca   b. sea lion
   c. narwhal   d. manta ray

SCORE

....

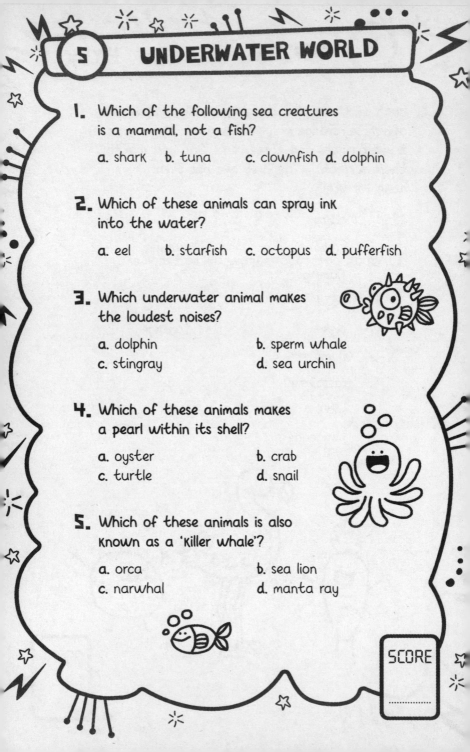

1. Which of the following trees produces acorns?

    a. lemon   b. oak   c. apple   d. pine

2. How many different oceans are there on Earth?

    a. seven   b. fifteen   c. one   d. five

3. What do tadpoles grow up to become?

    a. frogs   b. slugs   c. crickets   d. snails

4. Which of these animals has sharp, pointed spines all over its body?

    a. rat   b. honey badger
    c. porcupine   d. mole

5. Which of the following plants is important for making bread?

    a. dandelion   b. rose   c. wheat   d. thistle

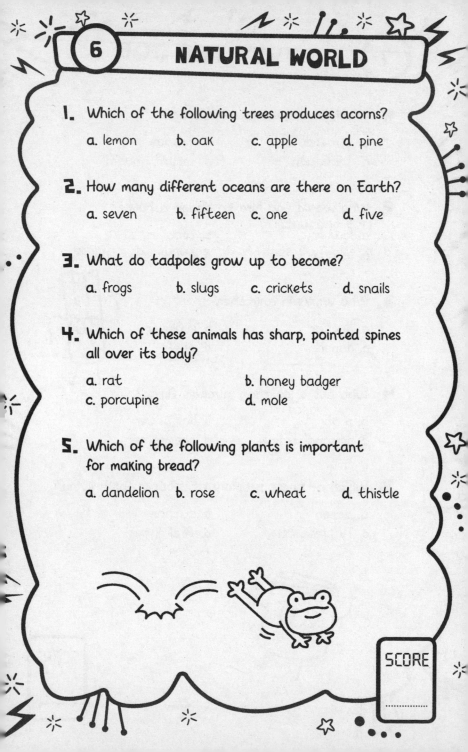

SCORE

1. Which person works with books?

    a. gardener   b. librarian

    c. electrician   d. security guard

2. Who would you hire to design a house?

    a. lawyer   b. teacher

    c. architect   d. gardener

3. Who works in a kitchen?

    a. doctor   b. engineer

    c. dancer   d. chef

4. Who has a job that involves flying?

    a. pilot   b. bus driver

    c. personal trainer   d. seamstress

5. Which of these people writes books for a living?

    a. actor   b. author

    c. TV presenter   d. firefighter

SCORE

....

BIRD BRAINS

1. Which of the following birds has the largest wingspan?

    a. robin   b. albatross c. eagle   d. owl

2. Which of these birds is unable to fly?

    a. dove   b. kingfisher c. penguin   d. sparrow

3. Which bird impresses the females of its kind by displaying its tail feathers?

    a. peacock b. dove   c. chicken   d. flamingo

4. Which bird is known for its large beak and throat, which it uses to collect fish?

    a. ostrich   b. woodpecker
    c. duck   d. pelican

5. Which bird is nocturnal (active at night instead of during the day)?

    a. seagull
    b. tawny owl
    c. stork
    d. heron

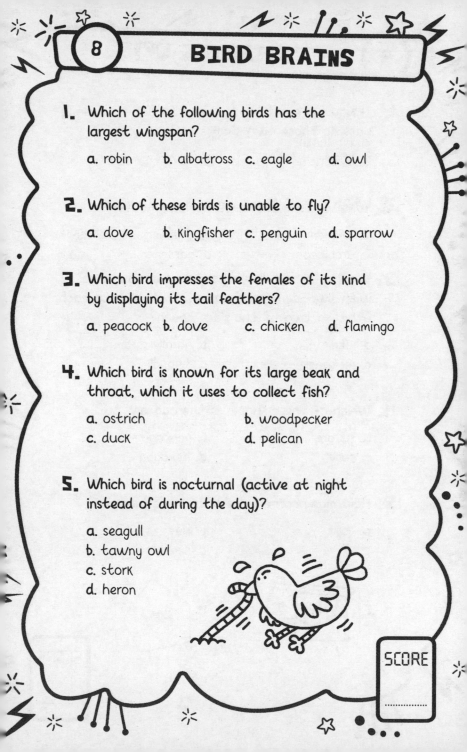

SCORE

SHAPING UP!

1. If you have a triangle and a square, how many sides do those two shapes have in total?

    a. three   b. four   c. seven   d. nine

2. Which one of these shapes has four sides?

    a. diamond   b. pentagon   c. circle   d. hexagon

3. Which of the following shapes can you make with two identical squares placed next to each other so two of the sides touch?

    a. kite   b. parallelogram
    c. rectangle   d. triangle

4. Which of these shapes is the odd one out?

    a. square   b. pentagon
    c. cube   d. hexagon

5. How many corners are there on a hexagon?

    a. four   b. five
    c. six   d. seven

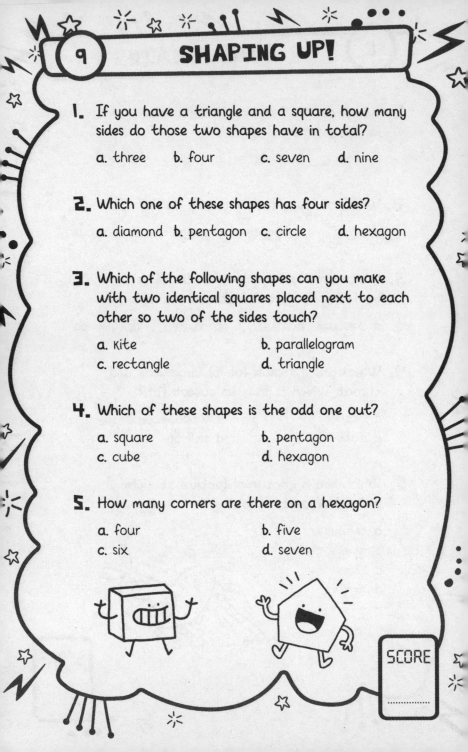

SCORE

MONTHS IN NUMBERS

Can you draw lines to match each month to the number of days that it has?

January	28 or 29
February	30
March	30
April	30
May	30
June	31
July	31
August	31
September	31
October	31
November	31
December	31

JANUARY

SCORE
....

TIME TEASERS

1. How many days are there in a leap year?

a. 365   b. 363   c. 425   d. 366

2. How many months are there in one and a half years?

a. 18   b. 21   c. 14   d. 23

3. How many hours are there in two days?

a. 35   b. 48   c. 60   d. 27

4. In which month is the middle day of the year?

a. July   b. March   c. October   d. May

5. How many seconds are there in three minutes?

a. 240   b. 600   c. 180   d. 120

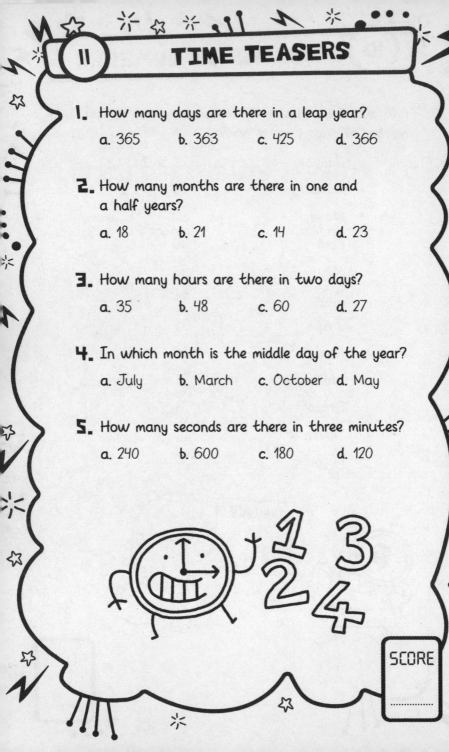

SCORE

....

STORE TOURS

Can you link each of the following types of store to an item you might expect to find inside?

STORE	SHOPPING LIST
bakery	bread
butcher	cabbage
delicatessen	cheese
fishmonger	cough syrup
florist	lobster
greengrocer	pencil case
pharmacy	steak
post office	stamps
stationer	tulips

SCORE

....

FLOWER POWER

1. Which of these flowers is well-known for its pleasant smell?

   a. sunflower   b. dahlia   c. rose   d. orchid

2. Which of these flowers shares its name with a musical instrument?

   a. daisy   b. viola   c. dahlia   d. gerbera

3. What is the name of the fine powder that forms inside flower heads?

   a. nectar   b. petal   c. stamen   d. pollen

4. Which of these would you need to plant if you wanted to grow a daffodil?

   a. seed   b. twig   c. bulb   d. bark

5. Which of these flowers is sometimes made into a chain by children?

   a. marigold   b. tulip   c. lily   d. daisy

SCORE

SCHOOL SUBJECTS

It's time to brush up on your school subjects. Draw lines to match each of the following topics to the correct school subject.

acting	art
biology	drama
exercise	English
faith	geography
French	gym
grammar	history
landscapes	languages
painting	mathematics
rhythm	music
shapes	religious studies
the Romans	science

2 + 2 =

SCORE

....

SCIENCE SUSSED

1. Which of these materials would be attracted to a magnet?

a. wood   b. plastic   c. paper   d. iron

2. If the Sun is shining on you from the east, which direction is your shadow pointing in?

a. north   b. east   c. south   d. west

3. What is the name of the gas that we need to take from the air every time we breathe in?

a. helium   b. oxygen   c. argon   d. steam

4. If you drop a heavy book and a light book from the same height at the same time, which will fall fastest?

a. heavy book   b. light book

c. either   d. they'll fall at the same speed

5. Which of these objects would definitely not float in a swimming pool?

a. a coin   b. a wooden block

c. a ping-pong ball   d. an empty water bottle

SCORE

....

ODD ONE OUT

Which is the odd one out in each of these rows? Do you know why?

1.	HOT	COLD	WARM	SLOW
2.	SUN	HAIL	SLEET	SNOW
3.	BICYCLE	BUS	TRICYCLE	SKATE-BOARD
4.	HAND	MOON	FACE	FOOT
5.	TOUCH	SMELL	THINK	SIGHT
6.	SWIM	RUN	WALK	JOG

SCORE
....

1. Which of these is a fruit, not a vegetable?

   a. cabbage   b. cauliflower

   c. tomato   d. green beans

2. Which of these vegetables grows underground?

   a. watercress   b. potato

   c. green bean   d. lettuce

3. Which one of these is a fungus, not a vegetable?

   a. broccoli   b. cabbage

   c. carrot   d. mushroom

4. Which vegetable grows in a pod?

   a. radish   b. pea   c. beetroot   d. asparagus

5. What is the name for the part of broccoli that is usually eaten?

   a. seeds   b. leaves

   c. root   d. flower buds

SCORE

....

3

RED, GREEN, BLUE

Each of these nine things is usually a shade of red, green or blue. There are three reds, three greens and three blues. Can you match them correctly?

cherry

crimson   red

cyan

emerald

lime   green

olive

ruby

sapphire   blue

navy

SCORE

....

AFRICAN ANIMALS

1. What are young lions usually called?

  a. pups   b. Kittens   c. cubs   d. cats

2. Which animal has the longest neck?

  a. elephant   b. mongoose
  c. tortoise   d. giraffe

3. Which group of animals is Known as a 'pride'?

  a. ostriches b. warthogs c. lions   d. buffalo

4. Which of the following can sprint faster than any other mammal on Earth?

  a. cheetah b. zebra   c. leopard d. rhinoceros

5. Which of the following animals is Known for its long trunk?

  a. crocodile   b. meerkat
  c. elephant   d. hippopotamus

SCORE

....

Can you match each item of food below to the correct shade?

broccoli	brown
butter	green
coffee	orange
ham	pink
milk	purple
red cabbage	red
tangerine	white
tomato	yellow

Chomp!

SCORE
....

DISNEY DECISIONS

1. Which movie tells the story of Simba and his father, Mufasa?

    a. *Frozen*

    c. *Cinderella*

    b. *The Lion King*

    d. *Snow White and the Seven Dwarfs*

2. Who is the central character in Disney's *The Little Mermaid*?

    a. Abby   b. Mary   c. Ariel   d. Samantha

3. In which movie does Baloo sing 'The Bare Necessities'?

    a. *The Jungle Book*

    c. *Moana*

    b. *Finding Nemo*

    d. *Coco*

4. Who is the main character in *Tangled*?

    a. Snow White

    c. Cinderella

    b. Belle

    d. Rapunzel

5. What type of toy is Woody in the *Toy Story* series?

    a. cowboy doll

    c. space ranger

    b. teddy bear

    d. motorized car

SCORE

HOME SWEET HOME

Can you match these animals to the places they call home?

badger	burrow
bee	den
bird	sett
dog	drey
fish	hive
fox	kennel
horse	nest
rabbit	sea
spider	stable
pig	sty
squirrel	web

SCORE

....

1. Which animal carries its home on its back?

    a. slug   b. grasshopper   c. mole   d. snail

2. Where do earthworms make their home?

    a. soil   b. sand   c. leaves   d. ponds

3. Which insect does a 'waggle dance' to show it has found nectar-rich flowers?

    a. butterfly b. fruit fly   c. bee   d. beetle

4. Which insect lays scent trails to help the rest of its group to find food?

    a. cricket   b. mosquito   c. aphid   d. ant

5. Which of these plants grows best in moist, shady areas?

    a. sunflower
    b. moss
    c. palm tree
    d. rose

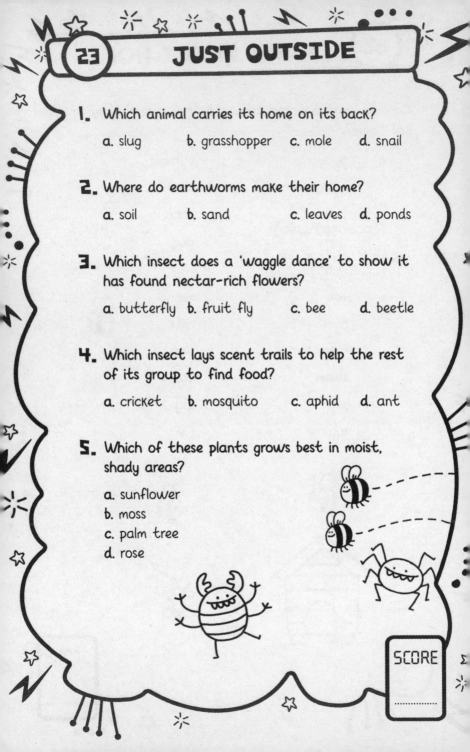

SCORE

....

BRILLIANT BOOKS

Take a look at this list of famous children's books.
See if you can match them with their authors.

Alice's Adventures in
Wonderland

A. A. Milne

Charlie and the
Chocolate Factory

Beatrix Potter

Harry Potter and
the Deathly Hallows

C. S. Lewis

How the Grinch Stole
Christmas

Dr Seuss

The House at
Pooh Corner

Enid Blyton

The Lion, the Witch
and the Wardrobe

J. K. Rowling

The Magic Faraway Tree

Lewis Carroll

The Tale of Peter Rabbit

Roald Dahl

SCORE

....

1. How many continents make up the world?

   a. 4   b. 7   c. 9   d. 10

2. Where would you have a chance of seeing a polar bear in the wild?

   a. Australia   b. Antarctica

   c. The Arctic   d. Egypt

3. Which continent is the island of Madagascar part of?

   a. Africa   b. Europe   c. Asia   d. South America

4. Which country is often said to be shaped like a boot?

   a. Ireland   b. Canada

   c. South Africa   d. Italy

5. Kangaroos are associated with which country?

   a. Mexico   b. India   c. Scotland   d. Australia

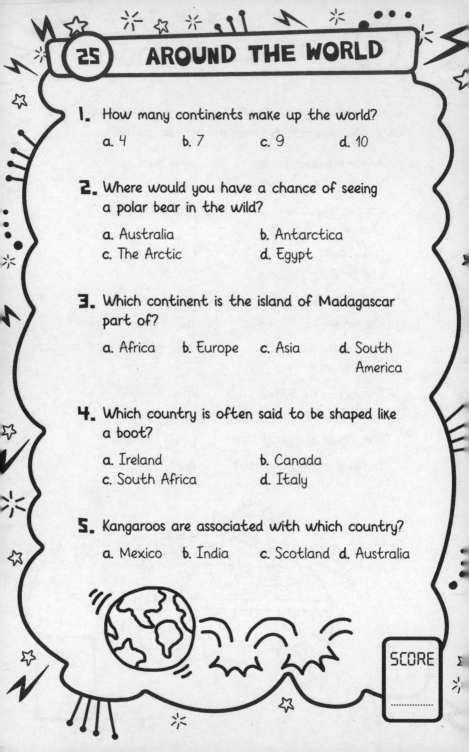

SCORE

....

TRACKING TIME

Can you draw lines to match each of these time periods to its correct length?

a century	1,000 years
a day	10 years
a decade	100 years
an hour	24 hours
a millennium	60 minutes
a minute	60 seconds
a month	seven days
a week	28 to 31 days
a year	365 to 366 days

SCORE

....

COMIC-BOOK HEROES

1. What material is Superman's main weakness?

a. salt   b. Kryptonite

c. fire   d. calcite

2. Which city does Batman protect?

a. London   b. Barcelona

c. Moscow   d. Gotham City

3. What is special about Captain America's shield?

a. it is shaped like a bird

b. it has a large 'A' on it

c. it is almost indestructible

d. it is made of high-quality cardboard

4. What weapon does Thor carry with him?

a. laser gun   b. spade

c. hammer   d. sword

5. What is The Hulk's main power?

a. flying   b. superhuman strength

c. invisibility   d. X-ray vision

SCORE

....

ON THE FARM

1. If a farmer tells you that an animal is a cow, which of the following is definitely NOT true?

    a. it lives in a field   **b.** it is female

    c. it is male   **d.** it eats grass

2. What is the name for the structure that pigs are kept in?

    a. barn   **b.** sty   **c.** kennel   **d.** tunnel

3. What is a baby chicken called?

    a. cockerel   **b.** rooster

    c. chick   **d.** hen

4. In what farm building are horses often kept overnight?

    a. pen   **b.** stable   **c.** hutch   **d.** horse house

5. Which of these is always produced by a dairy farm?

    a. meat   **b.** vegetables **c.** fruit   **d.** milk

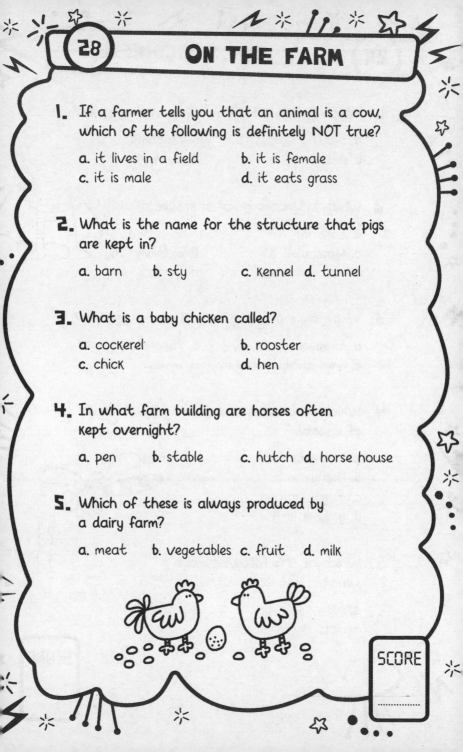

SCORE

....

1. Which insect lives in a colony with a queen?

   a. praying mantis   **b.** dragonfly

   c. ant   **d.** butterfly

2. What is the name for the type of skeleton that insects have?

   a. spine   **b.** exoskeleton

   c. endoskeleton   **d.** bionic

3. What type of mosquito will never bite you?

   a. tired ones   **b.** females

   c. ones that have fed **d.** males

4. Which of these is one of the largest types of insect?

   a. carpenter ant

   b. firefly

   c. marsh mosquito

   d. goliath beetle

5. Which of the following must termites eat to survive?

   a. soil   **b.** insects

   c. moss   **d.** wood

SCORE

....

HABITATS

Can you draw a line between the animal and the habitat where you would be most likely to find them?

bat	Antarctic
camel	Arctic
deer	bamboo forest
giant squid	cave
hermit crab	deep ocean
orangutan	desert
panda	rainforest
penguin	rock pool
polar bear	woodland

SCORE

....

1. How many strings does a typical acoustic guitar have?

a. 3   b. 6   c. 7   d. 10

2. Which of these is a brass instrument?

a. piano   b. harp
c. trumpet   d. drum

3. Which one of these instruments does not have strings?

a. violin   b. cello   c. flute   d. piano

4. Which of the following is also known as a mouth organ?

a. harmonica   b. banjo
c. triangle   d. piano

5. Which of these percussion instruments makes a loud sound similar to that of a bell?

a. snare drum   b. tambourine
c. gong   d. maracas

SCORE

....

Each of these nine things is usually a shade of purple, yellow or black. There are three purples, three yellows and three blacks. Can you match them correctly?

amethyst

banana   purple

charcoal

ebony

lemon   yellow

magenta

mauve

midnight   black

mustard

SCORE

....

Draw lines to match each of the baby animals to their parent.

calf	bear
chick	cat
cub	chicken
cygnet	cow
duckling	deer
fawn	dog
foal	duck
gosling	goose
joey	horse
kitten	kangaroo
lamb	owl
owlet	pig
piglet	sheep
puppy	swan

SCORE

WILD WEATHER

1. What is a hailstone made from?

    a. petals   b. sand   c. ice   d. wind

2. What is the middle of a hurricane known as?

    a. foot   b. eye   c. elbow   d. face

3. Which of these words describes a severe snowstorm?

    a. wind   b. blizzard   c. tornado   d. rain

4. Which of these is a type of 'precipitation'?

    a. rain   b. wind   c. dust   d. sunshine

5. What is the name given to somebody who studies or forecasts the weather?

    a. an observationer   b. a windy person
    c. a meteorologist   d. a weatherophile

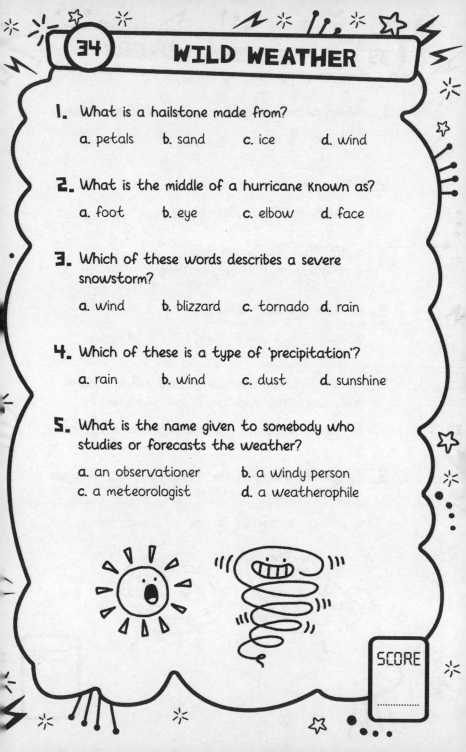

SCORE

....

I. Which of these foods is collected from beehives?

a. sugar   b. cake   c. honey   d. syrup

2. What sort of food does an omnivore eat?

a. meat, fruit and vegetables
b. only meat
c. only fruit and vegetables
d. only eggs, milk, cheese and bread

3. A raisin is a dried what?

a. plum   b. prune   c. fig   d. grape

4. Which of these utensils is most widely used in Asian countries such as Japan and China?

a. knife   b. fork   c. chopsticks   d. salad spoon

5. Spaghetti, macaroni and fettuccine are all types of what food?

a. pasta   b. bread   c. rice   d. cereal

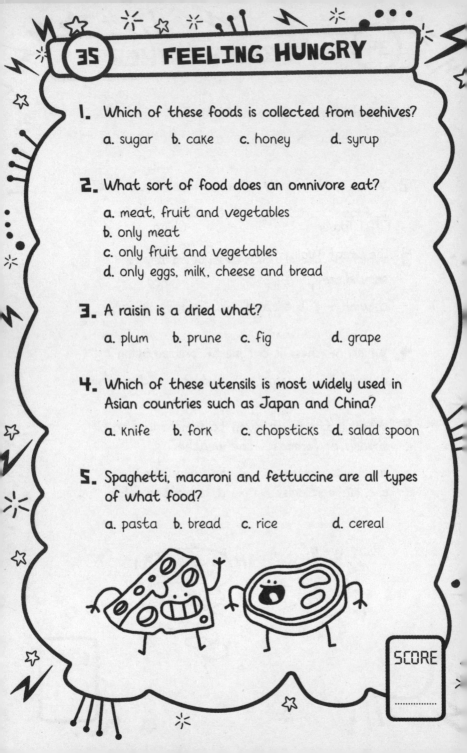

SCORE

....

FAMOUS LANDMARKS

Can you match each of these famous landmarks to its country? Leave any you are unsure about until last, as you may be able to work them out from the options that are left.

The Acropolis	Australia
Eiffel Tower	China
The Great Wall	Egypt
The Leaning Tower of Pisa	France
Machu Picchu	Greece
The Sphinx	India
St Basil's Cathedral	Italy
Statue of Liberty	Peru
Stonehenge	Russia
Sydney Opera House	United Kingdom
Taj Mahal	United States

Hello!

Bonjour!

SCORE

....

1. What type of ball, which is usually white, is covered in small dimples?

   a. tennis ball   **b.** softball

   c. baseball   **d.** golf ball

2. How many events are there in a triathlon?

   a. 3   **b.** 5   **c.** 7   **d.** 10

3. In which of these sports is the word 'love' used to indicate a score of zero?

   a. tennis   **b.** volleyball

   c. hockey   **d.** basketball

4. Which of these games is played in a swimming pool?

   a. croquet   **b.** water polo

   c. pool   **d.** netball

5. In which sport would you hit a shuttlecock?

   a. athletics

   b. ice hockey

   c. badminton

   d. football

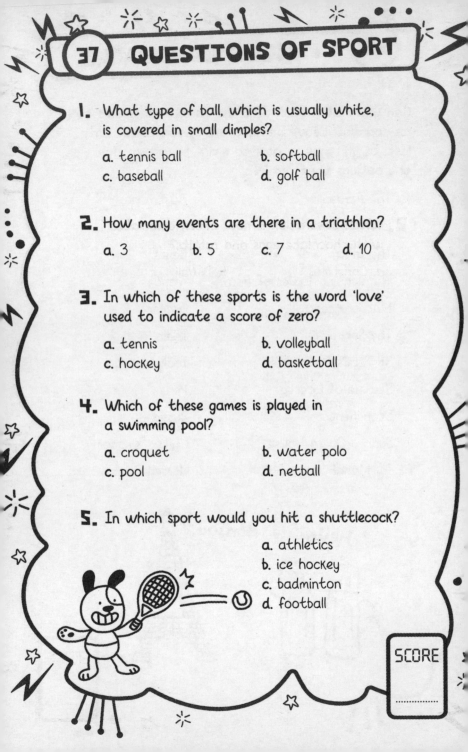

SCORE

....

CELEBRATIONS

1. What celebration of love takes place on the 14th of February, every year?

   a. Harvest Day
   c. Spring Day
   b. Valentine's Day
   d. Easter Day

2. Which celebration is now often associated with chocolate eggs and rabbits?

   a. Christmas
   c. Easter
   b. Diwali
   d. New Year

3. Which of the following do Sydney, London and other major cities often use to celebrate the New Year?

   a. fireworks
   c. a large bonfire
   b. candles
   d. silence

4. On what day of the year do some children go trick-or-treating?

   a. Father's Day
   c. Midsummer Day
   b. Mother's Day
   d. Halloween

5. On what night is the Christmas season traditionally said to end?

   a. Third night
   c. Eighth night
   b. Fifth night
   d. Twelfth night

SCORE

....

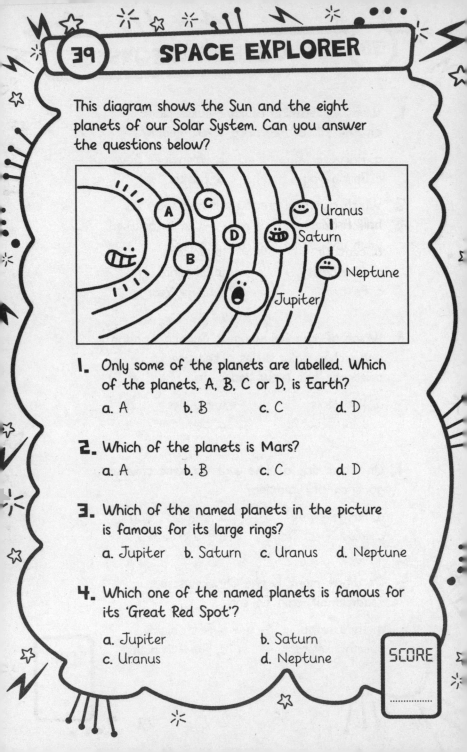

SPACE EXPLORER

This diagram shows the Sun and the eight planets of our Solar System. Can you answer the questions below?

A   C
D
B

Uranus
Saturn
Neptune
Jupiter

1. Only some of the planets are labelled. Which of the planets, A, B, C or D, is Earth?

a. A   b. B   c. C   d. D

2. Which of the planets is Mars?

a. A   b. B   c. C   d. D

3. Which of the named planets in the picture is famous for its large rings?

a. Jupiter   b. Saturn   c. Uranus   d. Neptune

4. Which one of the named planets is famous for its 'Great Red Spot'?

a. Jupiter   b. Saturn
c. Uranus   d. Neptune

SCORE

....

1. In myths, which creature do some humans change into when they see a full moon?

    a. fairy   b. werewolf c. dragon   d. vampire

2. Which mythical creature is half woman, half fish?

    a. centaur   b. unicorn

    c. mermaid   d. phoenix

3. Which mythical bird is said to rise from the ashes of a fire?

    a. phoenix b. roc   c. hawk   d. pigeon

4. Which mythical creature is half horse, half man?

    a. centaur   b. unicorn

    c. leprechaun   d. banshee

5. Which of the following is an enormous mythical sea creature?

    a. fawn

    b. whale

    c. Medusa

    d. Kraken

SCORE

....

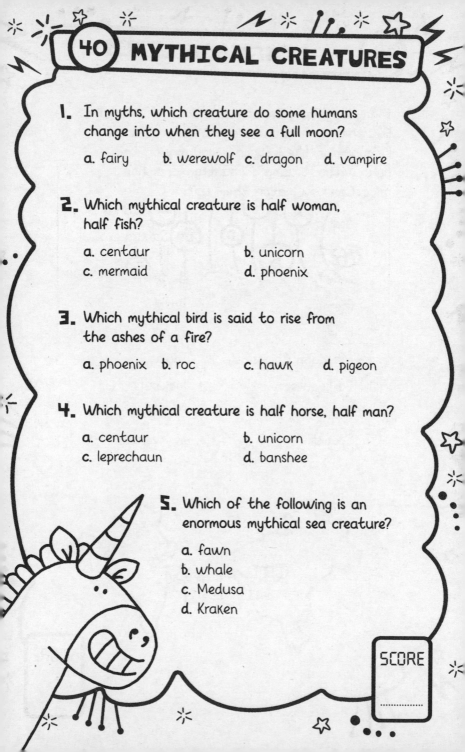

LANGUAGE LINES

Many languages are spoken in lots of countries, but there is only one way to connect each language on the left to a country on the right without using a country more than once. Can you match them up?

Arabic	Australia
English	Austria
French	Belarus
German	Brazil
Hindi	Egypt
Mandarin Chinese	India
Portuguese	Mexico
Russian	Singapore
Spanish	Switzerland

SCORE

....

1. What is the name given to an animal that eats other animals?

a. predator   b. product   c. prey   d. prince

2. What is the name for small ice crystals that form on the ground when the temperature falls below freezing?

a. frost   b. mud   c. snow   d. puddles

3. If an animal is described as a 'canine', what sort of animal is it?

a. a cat   b. a mouse   c. a dog   d. a horse

4. What is the regular movement of water in the sea called?

a. migration   b. solution
c. the tide   d. the flowing

5. Which of these natural features might produce lava?

a. a river   b. a tree
c. a canyon   d. a volcano

SCORE

....

CAPITAL MATCH

Let's take a quick trip around the world to see if you can match these twelve capital cities to their countries.

Beijing	Australia
Berlin	Austria
Brussels	Belgium
Cairo	Canada
Canberra	China
London	Egypt
Ottawa	France
Paris	Germany
Rome	Italy
Tokyo	Japan
Vienna	United Kingdom
Washington, DC	United States of America

G'day! Ciao!

SCORE

....

FAIRY TALES

1. In *The Three Little Pigs*, what does the first little pig build their house out of?

   a. plastic   b. wood   c. straw   d. bricks

2. In the classic story, what does Cinderella leave behind as she runs away from the ball?

   a. a book   b. glass slipper
   c. her dog   d. sunglasses

3. What did Rapunzel use to help the prince climb up the tower?

   a. rope   b. clothes   c. stairs   d. her hair

4. Whose house did Goldilocks enter uninvited?

   a. the three blind mice
   b. the three little pigs
   c. the three bears
   d. the three brothers

5. Where is *Aladdin* set?

   a. Western Europe
   b. Northern Europe
   c. Arabia
   d. South America

SCORE

NATIONALITIES

Can you draw lines to match each of the following nationalities to the correct country?

American	Denmark
British	Finland
Danish	Greece
Dutch	Ireland
Finnish	Netherlands
Greek	Peru
Irish	Spain
Peruvian	Switzerland
Spanish	Thailand
Swiss	United Kingdom
Thai	United States

SCORE

....

BONY BITS

1. How many bones are there in a typical adult human body?

a. 700   b. 206   c. 56   d. 500

2. Which set of bones forms a protective area over the heart and chest?

a. ribcage   b. scapula
c. phalanges   d. spine

3. What is the name of the bony structure that makes up the head?

a. patella   b. fibula   c. skull   d. jaw

4. Where in your body is your funny bone?

a. elbow   b. knee   c. toe   d. finger

5. Which bones form a structure that carries the weight of your head, torso and arms?

a. skull   b. femur   c. shin   d. spine

Blah blah blah!

SCORE
....

REPTILES

1. Which of the following has the ability to change the appearance of its skin?

    a. alligator   b. anaconda

    c. skink   d. chameleon

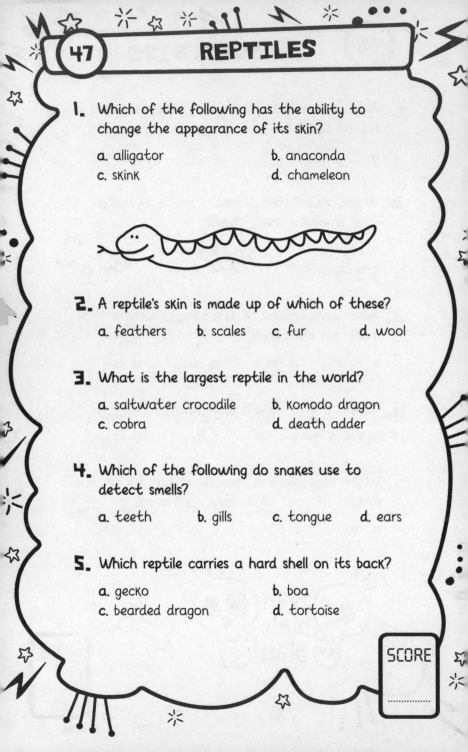

2. A reptile's skin is made up of which of these?

    a. feathers   b. scales   c. fur   d. wool

3. What is the largest reptile in the world?

    a. saltwater crocodile   b. Komodo dragon

    c. cobra   d. death adder

4. Which of the following do snakes use to detect smells?

    a. teeth   b. gills   c. tongue   d. ears

5. Which reptile carries a hard shell on its back?

    a. gecko   b. boa

    c. bearded dragon   d. tortoise

SCORE

....

TREES AND SEEDS

How much do you know about trees and their seeds? Let's find out! See if you can match each of the following seeds to the correct trees by writing their names in the spaces below.

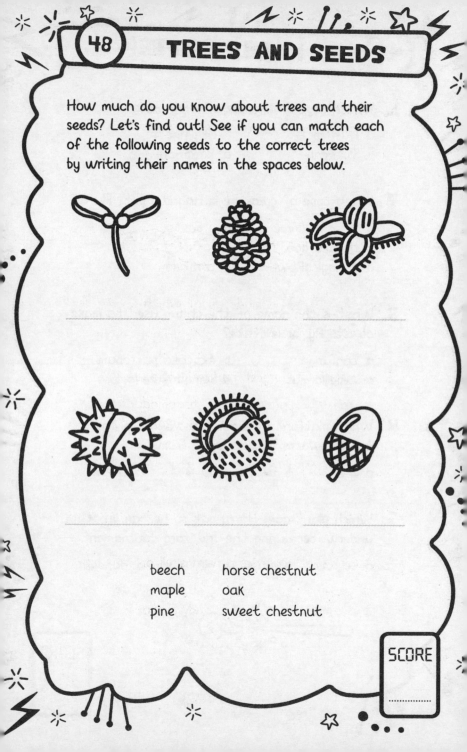

beech   horse chestnut
maple   oak
pine   sweet chestnut

SCORE

HARRY POTTER

1. Which Hogwarts house is Harry placed into?

 a. Hufflepuff b. Gryffindor
 c. Slytherin d. Ravenclaw

2. What type of creature is Hagrid's 'pet', Fluffy?

 a. a giant three- b. a basilisk
 headed dog
 c. a magical owl d. a dragon

3. What is the name of the charm used to make objects fly, or levitate?

 a. confundo b. expecto patronum
 c. expelliarmus d. wingardium leviosa

4. Which platform at King's Cross Station does the Hogwarts Express leave from?

 a. 8 ½ b. 9 ¾ c. 10 ¼ d. 12 ¾

5. Which plant does Harry eat so he can breathe underwater during the Triwizard Tournament?

 a. seaweed b. grass c. gillyweed d. dandelion

SCORE

Some countries have an official 'national animal' to represent them. Can you draw lines to match up these creatures with the correct countries?

bald eagle

bear

bull

koi carp

Bengal tiger

giant panda

golden eagle

kangaroo

kiwi

lion

Australia

China

India

Japan

Kenya

Mexico

New Zealand

Russia

Spain

United States

SCORE

1. What is the name of the process in which water changes from liquid to gas?

a. evaporation   b. precipitation
c. raining   d. draining

2. Water vapour in the air turns into droplets that form clouds via what process?

a. precipitation   b. fluffing
c. condensation   d. run-off

3. In which of the following might water naturally collect as part of the water cycle?

a. bathtub   b. bottle
c. umbrella   d. river

4. Which of the following is needed for the water cycle to take place?

a. the Sun   b. power stations
c. beaches   d. acid rain

5. What is it called when water soaks into the ground?

a. disturbation
b. dancing
c. infiltration
d. cycling

SCORE

....

WHERE ON EARTH?

Are you confident with countries and continents? Let's find out. There are two countries that belong in each of these continents. Can you draw lines to match them up correctly?

Argentina	Africa
Australia	
Brazil	Asia
Canada	
China	Europe
Ethiopia	
France	North America
India	
Morocco	Oceania
New Zealand	
United Kingdom	South America
United States	

SCORE

POND LIFE

1. Which animal builds dams to form a pond that protects its den?

   a. mouse   b. frog   c. sparrow d. beaver

2. Which best describes a pond?

   a. large body of salt water
   b. an area of fast-moving water
   c. a small body of still water
   d. water with regular waves

3. Which of these birds is most likely to be found living around a pond?

   a. duck   b. seagull   c. hawk   d. pigeon

4. Which of these animals can walk on water?

   a. frogs   b. pond skater c. swan   d. deer

5. Which of these animals does not start off as a tadpole?

   a. dragonfly b. newt
   c. frog   d. toad

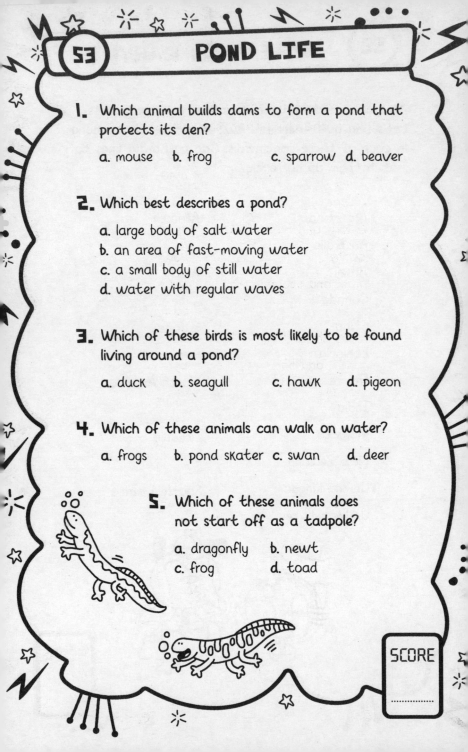

SCORE

....

Draw lines to match each of these units, or pairs of units, to the thing that they measure.

acre	area
calorie	distance
Celsius and Fahrenheit	energy
decibel	power
gram and stone	pressure
knot	sound level
kilometre and mile	temperature
pascal and bar	time
second	weight
watt	wind speed

SCORE

....

1. How long ago did most dinosaurs roam Earth?

    a. 160 to 1,600 years ago
    b. 6,000 to 16,000 years ago
    c. 10 million to 16 million years ago
    d. 66 million to 245 million years ago

2. Which dinosaur was named because of its head, which had three horns on it?

    a. Tyrannosaurus rex   b. Velociraptor
    c. Stegosaurus   d. Triceratops

3. The word 'dinosaur' is of Greek origin. What does it originally mean?

    a. terrible lizard   b. friendly alligator
    c. scary snake   d. fluffy dog

4. Which dinosaur had a remarkably long neck?

    a. Brachiosaurus   b. Megalosaurus
    c. Spinosaurus   d. Tyrannosaurus rex

5. How were baby dinosaurs born?

    a. they hatched from eggs
    b. they were brought by flying dinosaurs
    c. their mother gave birth to them
    d. there were no babies, so they died out

SCORE

Ten countries are listed below. Five are BIG, covering a large area of Earth's land surface. The other five are small. Tick the correct box for each one.

	BIG	SMALL
Australia		
Belgium		
Canada		
China		
Israel		
Jamaica		
Luxembourg		
Singapore		
Russia		
United States		

SCORE

....

TEETH

1. How many teeth do adult humans usually have?

    a. 16   b. 22   c. 32   d. 48

2. What do you call the long, sharp teeth which some snakes have?

    a. knives   b. biters   c. fangs   d. spiky teeth

3. Which are the last teeth to emerge into your mouth as you grow older?

    a. intelligent teeth   b. wisdom teeth
    c. final teeth   d. baby teeth

4. Traditionally, when might you most hope for a visit from the Tooth Fairy?

    a. at Christmas
    b. when you have lost a tooth
    c. when your first baby tooth appears
    d. when you brush twice a day for a week

5. What is the name of the bones your teeth are attached to?

    a. spine   b. skull
    c. jaw bones   d. nasal bone

SCORE

....

1. What is the name for the place where a river flows out into the ocean?

   a. foot   b. smile   c. mouth d. face

2. In which kind of natural environment would you expect to find a camel?

   a. rainforest   b. desert
   c. marshland   d. coral reef

3. What kind of tree is said to look like it is 'weeping'?

   a. oak   b. pine   c. willow d. birch

4. What is the name given to the molten rock that erupts from volcanoes?

   a. ash   b. lava   c. mulch d. water

5. What type of living thing is a toadstool?

   a. a plant   b. an animal
   c. a bacterium   d. a fungus

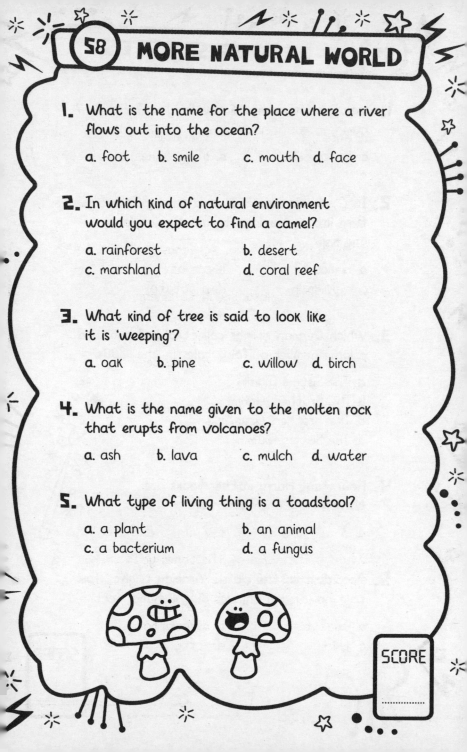

SCORE

....

FAMOUS STORIES

1. What is the name of the fairy in *Peter Pan*?

  a. Josie   b. Snickerdell
  c. Tinker Bell   d. Mary-Anne

2. In *Cinderella*, what does the Fairy Godmother turn into a carriage to get Cinderella to the ball?

  a. a mouse   b. a shoe
  c. a pumpkin   d. a potato

3. Which German siblings collected and published a large number of fairy tales in the 1800s?

  a. The Sisters Glamm
  b. The Brothers Grimm
  c. The Brothers Grummpy
  d. The Sisters Glumm

4. How many Harry Potter books are there in the original series?

  a. 3   b. 5   c. 7   d. 9

5. According to the classic 'Arabian Nights' folk tale, how many thieves did Ali Baba meet?

  a. ten   b. twenty
  c. thirty   d. forty

SCORE

....

1. Which of the following words can be used to describe an underground chamber?

a. marsh   b. beach   c. forest   d. cave

2. Which of these would describe a part of a river that suddenly drops straight down for some distance?

a. waterfall   b. extra river
c. canyon   d. spring

3. Which of the following words describes land that is surrounded by water on all sides?

a. desert   b. swamp
c. island   d. mountain

4. Which of these words can be described as a slow-moving mass, or river, of ice?

a. slope   b. glacier   c. tundra   d. sea

5. What name is given to a narrow valley between two hills or mountains?

a. gorge   b. rise   c. grassland   d. cliff

SCORE

....

1. For which of these activities would you use an easel and a palette?

    a. football   b. painting

    c. hiking   d. pottery

2. For which of these activities would you use a rake and a shovel?

    a. gymnastics   b. running

    c. origami   d. gardening

3. In which activity might you need to check you had the correct exposure?

    a. photography   b. karate

    c. golf   d. knitting

4. Which game has a king and a queen?

    a. monopoly   b. chess

    c. backgammon   d. uno

5. What would you be doing if you performed a sleight of hand?

    a. dancing

    b. magic

    c. making a paper plane

    d. singing

SCORE

....

1. What is an orchestra a group of?

    a. actors   b. singers

    c. musicians   d. dancers

2. What does a 'conductor' do?

    a. directs a musical performance

    b. takes pictures during the performance

    c. plays an instrument

    d. sells tickets to the performance

3. When the 'tempo' of the music is increased, what happens to it?

    a. it speeds up   b. it gets louder

    c. it slows down   d. it gets quieter

4. In a choir, what is a 'bass'?

    a. a high-pitched singer

    b. a soloist

    c. an accompanying instrument

    d. a low-pitched singer

5. What would you use a 'metronome' for?

    a. checking temperature   b. measuring distance

    c. keeping time   d. tuning an instrument

SCORE

....

1. What does 'www' at the start of web addresses stand for?

   a. We Want Words   b. While We Wait

   c. World Wide Web   d. Web Web Web

2. Which company developed the Android phone and tablet operating system?

   a. Yahoo   b. Google   c. Apache d. Bing

3. What is the main difference between a laptop and a desktop computer?

   a. a laptop is portable (can be carried around)

   b. a laptop is heavier

   c. a laptop costs less

   d. a laptop has a bigger screen

4. For digital file sizes, the abbreviation 'MB' stands for?

   a. megabytes   b. multi-biscuit

   c. molten-bread   d. millibytes

5. The Windows operating system is made by which large US company?

   a. Boeing   b. Microsoft

   c. AT&T   d. McDonald's

SCORE

....

1. Which of these is the world's tallest mountain?

   a. Everest　　　　　b. Kilimanjaro
   c. Snowdon　　　　d. Saint Elias

2. Which is the largest sandy desert in the world?

   a. Antarctica　　　b. Gobi
   c. Sahara　　　　　d. Mojave

3. Which of these countries has the longest coastline in the world?

   a. Russia　　　　　b. Australia
   c. Argentina　　　d. Canada

4. What is the largest country in the world, in terms of its land area?

   a. United States of America
   b. France
   c. Russia
   d. China

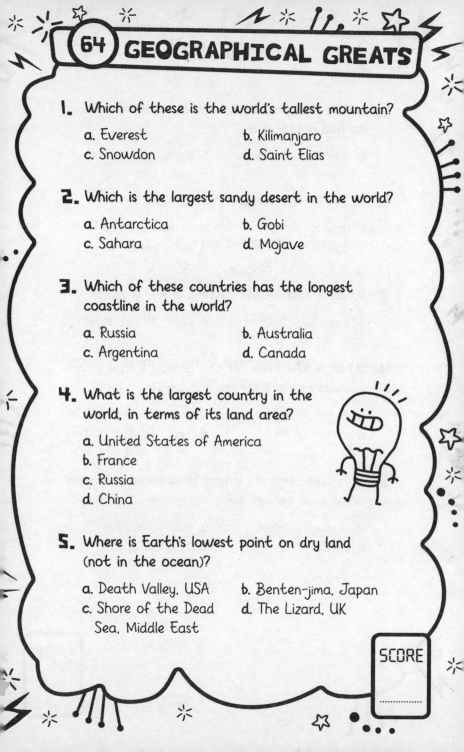

5. Where is Earth's lowest point on dry land (not in the ocean)?

   a. Death Valley, USA　　b. Benten-jima, Japan
   c. Shore of the Dead　　d. The Lizard, UK
   　 Sea, Middle East

SCORE

....

PLANTS

1. Inside which of these fruits would you expect to find a stone?

   a. melon   b. apricot   c. apple   d. pineapple

2. Which of the following plants eats insects?

   a. holly   b. venus fly trap
   c. dandelion   d. palm tree

3. What is the world's fastest growing plant?

   a. bamboo   b. cactus   c. ivy   d. sunflower

4. What is the term for the group of fruits that includes oranges, lemons and limes?

   a. bright fruits   b. sour fruits
   c. citrus fruits   d. zingy fruits

5. If a tree keeps its leaves throughout the year, what is it known as?

   a. autumnal tree   b. evergreen tree
   c. winter tree   d. deciduous tree

SCORE

Here are ten flags and ten countries. Use the symbols on each flag to help you work out which country it belongs to, then draw a line to match them up.

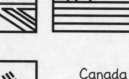

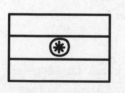

Canada
China
Greece
India
Israel
Japan
Morocco
South Korea
United Kingdom
United States

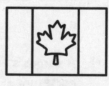

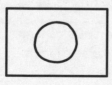

SCORE

....

1. Every day a farmer collects three eggs, and eats one. How many eggs are there at the end of the week?

    a. 10   b. 14   c. 18   d. 24

2. If there are four chickens, two pigs and one horse in a field, what is the total number of animal legs in that field?

    a. 10   b. 16   c. 20   d. 30

3. I am walking to the farm, and pass 35 sheep coming the other way, followed by two dogs, a farmer and five children. How many animals and people are walking to the farm?

    a. 1   b. 6   c. 43   d. 100

4. A farmer's field is only large enough to keep five horses in. If he wants to keep twenty horses, how many times larger does the field need to be?

    a. twice as large   b. three times as large
    c. four times as large   d. five times as large

5. Five cows produce enough milk to fill two large bottles each day. How many extra cows are needed to fill ten bottles each day?

    a. 5   b. 10
    c. 20   d. 40

SCORE

....

OVER THE RAINBOW

1. Which food is most commonly orange, but also has purple and white varieties?

a. oranges
b. pear
c. carrot
d. cabbage

2. Which flower is most associated with love and romance?

a. red rose
b. orange marigold
c. yellow daffodil
d. blue hyacinth

3. Which of these is also a traditional girl's name?

a. Red
b. Blue
c. Purple
d. Violet

4. Which of these is a type of vegetable?

a. indigo leek
b. red cucumber
c. green bean
d. blue onion

5. According to myths, what is said to be found at the end of the rainbow?

a. a phone-charger
b. sunglasses
c. a pot of gold
d. mud

SCORE

....

TWO BY TWO

Are you a budding zoologist, or do you know zilch about the animal kingdom? See if you can match up the names of males and females to the correct animal. The first is done for you.

animals	female	male
cattle	cow	billy
chickens	doe	boar
deer	ewe	bull
goats	hen	cob
horses	lioness	cockerel
lions	mare	lion
peafowl	nanny	peacock
pigs	peahen	ram
sheep	pen	stag
swans	sow	stallion

SCORE

1. What does a singer hold while performing?

a. speakers   b. a microphone
c. a vacuum cleaner   d. an amplifier

2. Which instrument has a bass version often used in a band?

a. piano   b. trumpet   c. drums   d. guitar

3. What is the term for a singer who performs alone, often without musical accompaniment?

a. chorister   b. soloist   c. busker   d. vocalist

4. If a piece of sheet music is marked at the top with 'presto', what would it mean?

a. as slowly as possible
b. only by magicians
c. at a very fast speed
d. on a tambourine

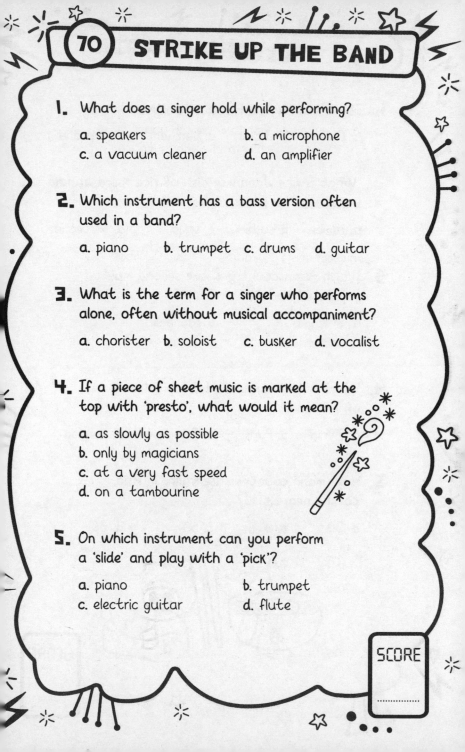

5. On which instrument can you perform a 'slide' and play with a 'pick'?

a. piano   b. trumpet
c. electric guitar   d. flute

SCORE

....

ALL ABOUT ASIA

1. The Great Wall is found in which country?

    a. China   b. Japan   c. Vietnam   d. Thailand

2. What is the Japanese dish of rice rolled around various other foods known as?

    a. ramen   b. sushi   c. soup   d. barbecue

3. Which Asian country is the second most populated country on Earth?

    a. Malaysia   b. Mongolia
    c. Cambodia   d. India

4. What is the name of the capital city of Thailand?

    a. Berlin   b. Paris   c. Bangkok   d. London

5. How many countries are there in Asia, to the nearest 10?

    a. 30   b. 40   c. 50   d. 60

SCORE

....

PLANT LIFE

1. Which of the following vegetables is often associated with Halloween?

a. pumpkin b. potato   c. radish   d. lettuce

2. Fill in the blanks: plants need .... and .... to create food.

a. bread and milk   b. water and sunlight
c. soil and clay   d. fruit and vegetables

3. Which of these plants is not a herb?

a. parsley b. thyme   c. cherry d. basil

4. Which of these fruits grows on trees?

a. strawberries   b. pineapples
c. apples   d. rhubarb

5. Which of the following is a root vegetable?

a. carrot b. lettuce   c. corn   d. asparagus

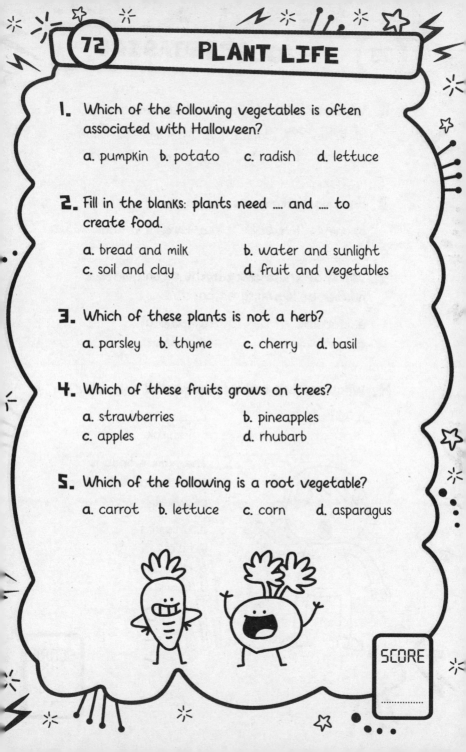

SCORE

....

1. Which of these things helps to bend parts of your body so you can walk and move?

   a. veins   b. muscles   c. palms   d. heart

2. How many stomachs does a cow have?

   a. one   b. two   c. three   d. four

3. Which of these creatures has the greatest number of legs?

   a. crocodile   b. spider
   c. centipede   d. kangaroo

4. What are the breathing organs of fish called?

   a. scales   b. fins   c. gills   d. eyes

5. The human body is made up of trillions of what?

   a. vitamins
   b. hairs
   c. cells
   d. bones

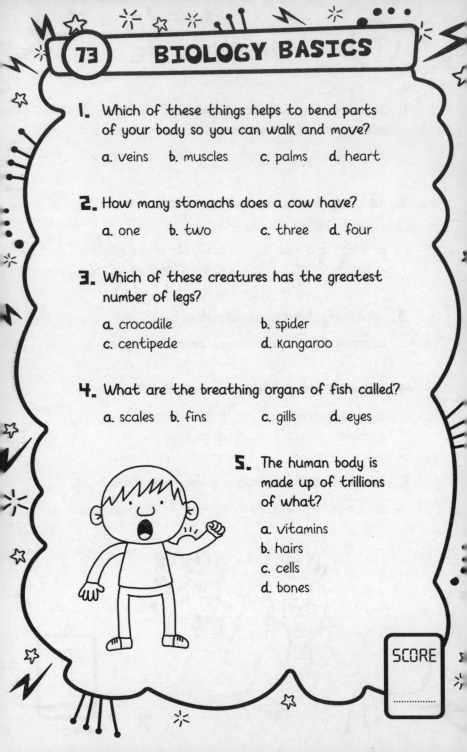

SCORE

....

ANIMAL LIVES

Different types of animal live for different amounts of time. Can you draw lines to match each of the following animals to the average time it might live? To give you an extra clue, in general, the smaller the animal is, the shorter its lifespan will be.

chimpanzee	10 days
elephant	25 days
fruit fly	150 days
guinea pig	5 years
honeybee	10 years
horse	25 years
male mosquito	50 years
sea turtle	70 years
wolf	100 years

When I was your age ....

SCORE
....

1. If you sleep for eight hours a night, roughly how much time is likely to be spent dreaming?

a. 5 minutes   b. 30 minutes
c. 2 hours   d. 6 hours

2. Which of these diseases is carried by mosquitoes?

a. chicken pox   b. bird flu
c. malaria   d. measles

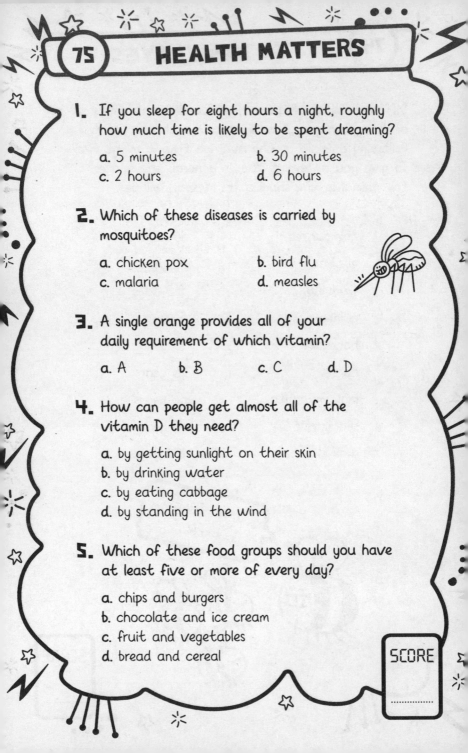

3. A single orange provides all of your daily requirement of which vitamin?

a. A   b. B   c. C   d. D

4. How can people get almost all of the vitamin D they need?

a. by getting sunlight on their skin
b. by drinking water
c. by eating cabbage
d. by standing in the wind

5. Which of these food groups should you have at least five or more of every day?

a. chips and burgers
b. chocolate and ice cream
c. fruit and vegetables
d. bread and cereal

SCORE

....

THE OLYMPICS

1. Where was the first Olympic Games held?

    a. Washington   **b.** Beijing

    c. Athens   **d.** Colorado

2. A hundred years ago, which of the following events was part of the Olympics?

    a. the egg-and-spoon   **b.** three-legged race

    c. tug-of-war   **d.** sack race

3. On average, how fast can an Olympic champion sprint the 100 metres race?

    a. 4 to 5 seconds   **b.** 9 to 10 seconds

    c. 14 to 15 seconds   **d.** 29 to 30 seconds

4. What do the the five rings in the Olympic logo represent?

    a. the five founding countries

    b. the five original athletics events

    c. the five continents

    d. the number of days it lasts

5. In 2012, which city became the first to host the Olympic games for a third time?

    a. Paris   **b.** London

    c. Los Angeles   **d.** Tokyo

SCORE

....

THE SUN

I. What is a sundial used for?

a. making food   b. collecting energy

c. telling the time   d. measuring distance

2. What is the energy that is collected from the Sun called?

a. solar power   b. hydroelectric power

c. wind power   d. natural gas

3. What type of object is the Sun?

a. a planet   b. an asteroid

c. a star   d. a moon

4. What is the Sun made of?

a. molten rock

b. boiling water

c. hot gas

d. a million lightbulbs

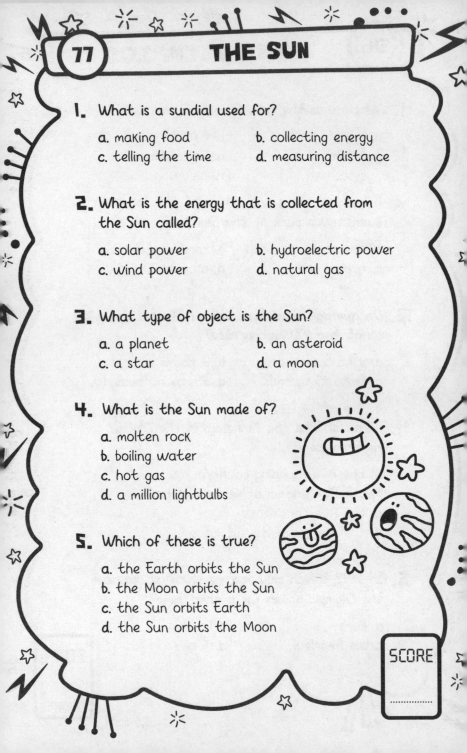

5. Which of these is true?

a. the Earth orbits the Sun

b. the Moon orbits the Sun

c. the Sun orbits Earth

d. the Sun orbits the Moon

SCORE

....

MIXING IT UP

1. Which of these two paints can you mix to create green?

a. red and blue   b. green and blue
c. yellow and blue   d. white and black

2. If you mix red and yellow paints, which of these is the result?

a. purple   b. pink   c. orange   d. blue

3. To make purple paint, which of these two paints can you mix together?

a. red and blue   b. red and green
c. green and blue   d. yellow and green

4. If you mix red and white paints, which of these is the result?

a. orange   b. light red
c. pink   d. light purple

5. Which of the following light combinations do TVs emit?

a. red, green and yellow
b. red, green and blue
c. green, yellow and blue
d. blue, red and yellow

SCORE
....

I. Which of these flightless birds is now extinct?

    a. dodo   b. emu   c. ostrich   d. penguin

2. Which large, elephant-like creature had a pair of huge, curved tusks and roamed Earth during the last Ice Age?

    a. rhinoceros   b. nellysaurus

    c. woolly mammoth   d. elephantus gigantus

3. There was once an Australian dog-like animal known as a Tasmanian tiger that could hop for short distances on its back legs. What other name was it known by?

    a. a plasticine   b. a thylacine

    c. a tigaroo   d. a kangatiger

4. The quagga, a type of zebra, lived in South Africa until the 1800s. Its back half was plain brown but what was on its front half?

    a. green spots   b. yellow and

                            brown checks

    c. orange stars   d. brown stripes

5. The great auk was a type of what?

    a. flightless bird   b. whale

    c. bird of prey   d. reptile

SCORE

....

RELIGION

1. Which of these religions involves praying to multiple gods, not just one?

a. Hinduism   b. Judaism
c. Christianity   d. Islam

2. What is the name of the building where Jewish people go to attend regular services?

a. shrine   b. synagogue
c. cathedral   d. mosque

3. Diwali is celebrated once a year. What is it the Hindu festival of?

a. cake   b. sleep   c. lights   d. elephants

4. What name is given to the Pope's ceremonial tall, white hat?

a. crown   b. beanie   c. bowler   d. mitre

5. Which of these symbols is most associated with Buddhism?

a. star
b. wheel
c. square
d. pyramid

SCORE

....

These prefixes, or first parts of words, are used to describe measurements and ways to store digital information. Can you sort them into order of increasing size? For example, if you think that kilo is bigger than milli, then you should place kilo further down the list than milli.

centi	giga
kilo	mega
milli	tera

SMALLEST

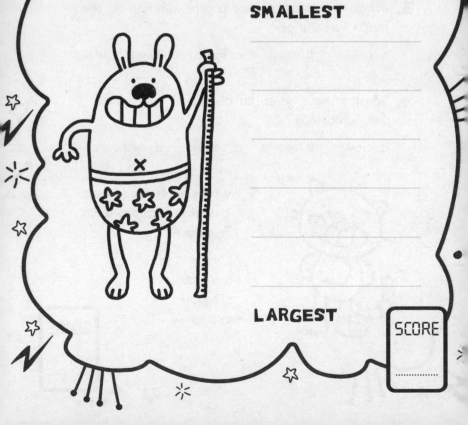

LARGEST

SCORE

....

MAKING IT UP

1. From which of these liquids is butter made?

    a. water   b. milk   c. orange juice d. cola

2. Which of these seeds is used to make chocolate?

    a. cacao   b. pumpkin c. sunflower   d. sesame

3. Which of these liquids is used to make roads?

    a. mercury   b. olive oil
    c. tar   d. egg white

4. Which of these objects is most likely to contain natural rubber?

    a. a car tyre   b. a speaker
    c. a pen   d. a ruler

5. Which metal makes up most of the content of many common silver-looking coins?

    a. silver   b. copper c. nickel   d. tin

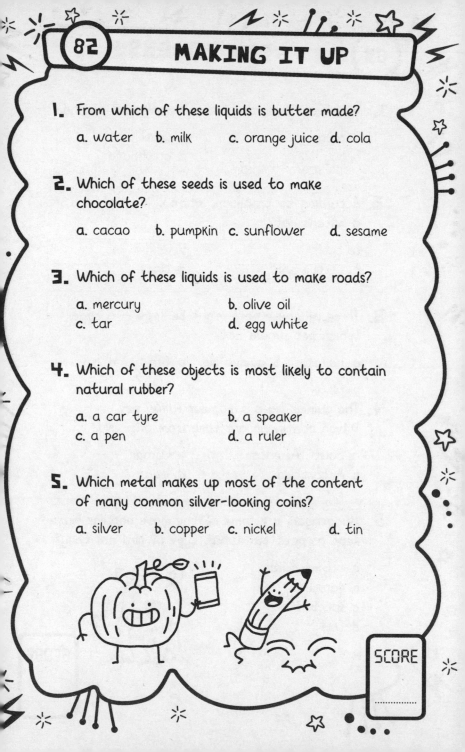

SCORE

PET POSERS

1. Which of these dog breeds usually has long hair?

a. retriever

b. dalmatian

c. pug

d. greyhound

2. According to tradition, what colour is a witch's cat?

a. tabby

b. white

c. tortoiseshell

d. black

3. Three of these pets might be kept in a cage. Which pet would not?

a. hamster

b. guinea pig

c. fish

d. rat

4. The guinea pig is a popular family pet. Which continent are they from originally?

a. South America

b. Europe

c. Antarctica

d. Asia

5. Budgerigars are some of the most popular birds kept as pets, but what type of bird are they?

a. hummingbird

b. parakeet

c. songbird

d. owl

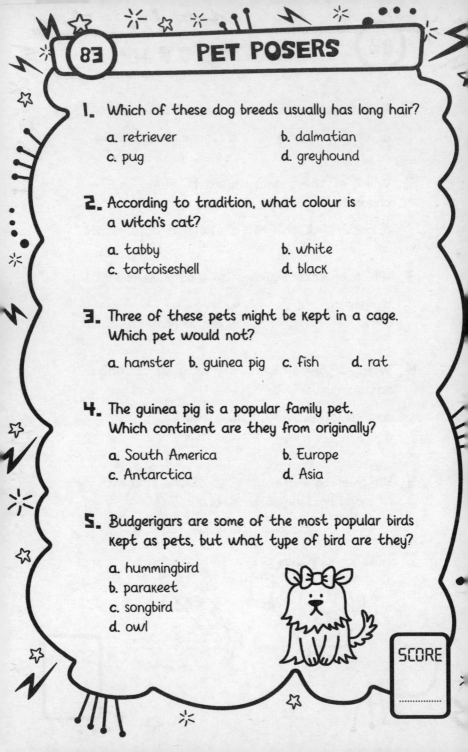

SCORE

....

A MIXED BAG

1. In the *Winnie-the-Pooh* stories, what is the name of Pooh's human friend?

a. Christopher Robin   b. Jennifer Lawrence
c. Justin Bieber   d. Beyoncé

2. Which of the following is not a suit in a normal deck of cards?

a. diamonds   b. hearts
c. spades   d. circles

3. Which legendary character stole from the rich and gave to the poor?

a. Buzz Lightyear   b. Robin Hood
c. Wolverine   d. Voldemort

4. What is the name of the building that the President of the United States lives in?

a. Buckingham Palace   b. The White House
c. 10 Downing Street   d. Strasbourg

5. Which country is famous for creating the croissant?

a. Germany   b. Japan
c. France   d. Mexico

SCORE
....

VOCAB VERIFIER

The English language has more than 150,000 words, but most adults only use around 20,000, which means there are always new ones to discover. See how many of these words you can match with the correct meaning. The first has been done for you. If you find this difficult, try looking the words up in a dictionary.

bonanza	a boat with two connected hulls
catamaran	a daydream, or being lost in thought
concoction	a sudden increase of good luck
euphoric	a fruit that's a bit like a tiny orange
isosceles	a large celebration
jamboree	a mix of various different ingredients
kumquat	a triangle with two sides of equal length
reverie	feeling really happy
sophistry	quirky or different in an amusing way
zany	the use of clever but false arguments

SCORE

....

I. How many world wars have there been?

    a. none   b. one   c. two   d. three

2. Who is the Victorian age (from 1837 to 1901) named after?

    a. Prince Charles   b. King John
    c. Princess Fiona   d. Queen Victoria

3. Which part of the world did the Vikings come from?

    a. Africa   b. Scandinavia
    c. South America   d. The Moon

4. In which country did the pharaohs live?

    a. Canada   b. Japan   c. Egypt   d. Wales

5. Who was the very first president of the United States?

    a. George Washington
    b. Winston Churchill
    c. Abraham Lincoln
    d. Harry Potter

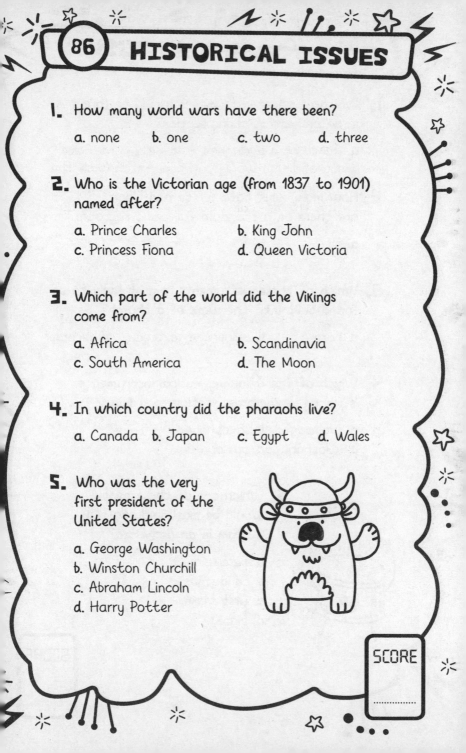

SCORE

1. Which of these instruments would be found in an orchestra's string section?

a. french horn b. clarinet   c. cello   d. flute

2. How many keys, both white and black, are there on a standard full piano keyboard?

a. 54   b. 63   c. 88   d. 100

3. Which of these instruments is most likely to be found built into the walls of a church?

a. harp   b. xylophone c. organ   d. recorder

4. Which of the following musical instruments is placed in the brass section of a band?

a. trombone   b. saxophone
c. xylophone   d. bassoon

5. Which one of these people would be most likely to play a drum in an orchestra?

a. percussionist
b. conductor
c. first violin
d. pianist

SCORE
....

GEOGRAPHY ROUND 2

1. What covers approximately 71 per cent of Earth's surface?

a. land   b. water   c. grass   d. sand

2. What is an animal or plant's natural home or environment known as?

a. apartment   b. cottage
c. lake   d. habitat

3. What is the world's largest and deepest ocean?

a. Atlantic   b. Pacific   c. Arctic   d. Indian

4. What is the imaginary dividing line that separates the northern and southern hemispheres called?

a. Line of longitude   b. Equator
c. Tropic of Capricorn   d. Tropic of Cancer

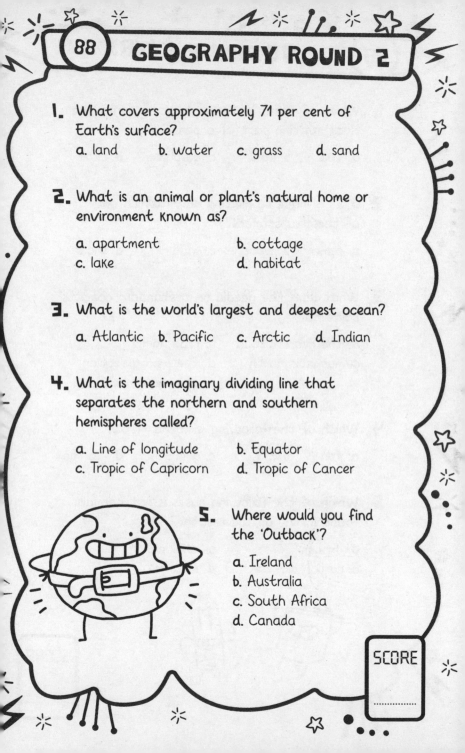

5. Where would you find the 'Outback'?

a. Ireland
b. Australia
c. South Africa
d. Canada

SCORE
....

SCIENCE EXTRA

1. Which of these materials typically forms the black, writing part of a pencil?

   a. lead   b. iron   c. graphite   d. chalk

2. Glass is made by melting down which one of these substances?

   a. cement   b. wood   c. sand   d. sugar

3. What does the needle on a standard compass point to?

   a. the nearest road   b. true north
   c. magnetic north   d. the next direction
                              you should head

4. Which of the following is not a metal?

   a. iron   b. tin   c. gold   d. granite

5. Which of the following gases is not normally found in the air we breathe?

   a. oxygen   b. ammonia
   c. carbon dioxide   d. nitrogen

SCORE
....

SPACE ACE

1. What is it called when the Moon passes behind Earth into its shadow?

    a. a tidal event   **b.** a lunar eclipse

    c. global warming   **d.** a solar eclipse

2. Which of the following is a dwarf planet?

    a. Jupiter   **b.** Earth   **c.** Mars   **d.** Pluto

3. Which of these instruments would you use to observe the Moon and stars?

    a. microscope   **b.** telescope

    c. stethoscope   **d.** kaleidoscope

4. Who was the first person to walk on the Moon?

    a. Elvis Presley   **b.** Yuri Gagarin

    c. Neil Armstrong   **d.** Tim Peake

5. Which country was the first to launch a human into space?

    a. Russia (known then as the USSR)

    b. United States

    c. China

    d. United Kingdom

SCORE

....

POPULATION SORTER

Can you sort the following countries into order of population (number of people) so that the country with the smallest population is at the top and the country with the biggest population is at the bottom?

Australia
China
Ireland
Japan
United Kingdom
United States

SMALLEST
BIGGEST

SCORE

....

1. Which of these famous sites was NOT built by the ancient Romans?

   a. The Colosseum   b. The Parthenon

   c. The Pantheon   d. Hadrian's Wall

2. Which of these was one of the Seven Wonders of the Ancient World?

   a. The Hanging Gardens of Babylon

   b. The Swinging Seat of Ephesus

   c. The Falling Temple of Olympia

   d. The Ugly House of Mesopotamia

3. Which Chinese dynasty dates back to around 1600 BC?

   a. Greek   b. Roman   c. Shang   d. Persian

4. Which of these is an ancient Greek coin?

   a. franc   b. lira   c. obol   d. pound

5. The Great Pyramid of Giza is the only one of the Seven Wonders of the Ancient World that is still standing. Where can it be found?

   a. France   b. Mexico

   c. Turkey   d. Egypt

SCORE

Can you draw lines to match each of the following people to the invention they are most associated with?

Ada Lovelace	battery
Alessandro Volta	computer program
Guglielmo Marconi	dishwasher
Hedy Lamarr	frequency hopping (used in Wi-Fi and GPS)
Johannes Gutenberg	Kevlar
Josephine Cochrane	lightbulb
Stephanie Kwolek	printing press
Thomas Edison	radio communication
Tim Berners-Lee	satellite propulsion system
Yvonne C. Brill	World Wide Web

SCORE

ALL
THE
ANSWERS

ANSWERS

QUIZ 1

plants:
carrot, dandelion, fern, garlic, holly

animals:
dolphin, horse, lion, kangaroo, zebra

QUIZ 2

1. d
2. a
3. d
4. a
5. a

QUIZ 3

1. c
2. d
3. a
4. c
5. a

QUIZ 4

white	cream, pearl, snow
orange	carrot, pumpkin, tangerine
pink	flamingo, piglet, raspberry

QUIZ 5

1. d
2. c
3. b
4. a
5. a

QUIZ 6

1. b
2. d, most people agree that there are five oceans: the Atlantic, Pacific, Indian, Arctic and Antarctic
3. a
4. c
5. c

QUIZ 7

1. b
2. c
3. d
4. a
5. b

QUIZ 8

1. b
2. c
3. a
4. d
5. b

ANSWERS

QUIZ 9

1. c
2. a
3. c
4. c, because it is a three-dimensional shape and the others are two-dimensional.
5. c

QUIZ 10

28 or 29: February
30: April, June, September, November
31: January, March, May, July, August, October, December

QUIZ 11

1. d
2. a
3. b
4. a
5. c

QUIZ 12

bakery	bread
butcher	steak
delicatessen	cheese
fishmonger	lobster
florist	tulips
greengrocer	cabbage
pharmacy	cough syrup
post office	stamps
stationer	pencil case

QUIZ 13

1. c
2. b
3. d
4. c
5. d

QUIZ 14

acting	drama
biology	science
exercise	gym
faith	religious studies
French	languages
grammar	English
landscapes	geography
painting	art
rhythm	music
shapes	mathematics
the Romans	history

ANSWERS

QUIZ 15

1. d
2. d
3. b
4. d
5. a

QUIZ 16

1. slow — all the others refer to temperatures

2. Sun — all the rest are cold, wet types of weather

3. bus — this is the only motorized method of transport

4. moon — the others are body parts

5. think — the others are basic senses that you have; think is not one of the senses

6. swim — all the rest are ways of moving on land

QUIZ 17

1. c
2. b
3. d
4. b
5. d

QUIZ 18

red	cherry, crimson, ruby
green	emerald, lime, olive
blue	cyan, sapphire, navy

QUIZ 19

1. c
2. d
3. c
4. a
5. c

QUIZ 20

broccoli	green
butter	yellow
coffee	brown
ham	pink
milk	white
red cabbage	purple
tangerine	orange
tomato	red

Chomp!

ANSWERS

QUIZ 21

1. b
2. c
3. a
4. d
5. a

QUIZ 22

badger	sett
bee	hive
bird	nest
dog	kennel
fish	sea
fox	den
horse	stable
rabbit	burrow
spider	web
pig	sty
squirrel	drey

QUIZ 23

1. d
2. a
3. c
4. d
5. b

QUIZ 24

Alice's Adventures in Wonderland: Lewis Carroll
Charlie and the Chocolate Factory: Roald Dahl
Harry Potter and the Deathly Hallows: J. K. Rowling
How the Grinch Stole Christmas: Dr Seuss
The House at Pooh Corner: A. A. Milne
The Lion, the Witch and the Wardrobe: C. S. Lewis
The Magic Faraway Tree: Enid Blyton
The Tale of Peter Rabbit: Beatrix Potter

QUIZ 25

1. b
2. c
3. a
4. d
5. d

QUIZ 26

a century   100 years
a day   24 hours
a decade   10 years
an hour   60 minutes
a millennium   1,000 years
a minute   60 seconds
a month   28 to 31 days
a week   seven days
a year   365 to 366 days (leap years
                have an extra day)

ANSWERS

QUIZ 27

1. b
2. d
3. c
4. c
5. b

QUIZ 28

1. c
2. b
3. c
4. b
5. d

QUIZ 29

1. c
2. b
3. d
4. d
5. d

QUIZ 30

bat	cave
camel	desert
deer	woodland
giant squid	deep ocean
hermit crab	rock pool
orangutan	rainforest
panda	bamboo forest
penguin	Antarctic
polar bear	Arctic

QUIZ 31

1. b
2. c
3. c
4. a
5. c

QUIZ 32

purple	amethyst, magenta, mauve
yellow	banana, lemon, mustard
black	charcoal, ebony, midnight

ANSWERS

QUIZ 33

calf	cow
chick	chicken
cub	bear
cygnet	swan
duckling	duck
fawn	deer
foa	horse
gosling	goose
joey	kangaroo
kitten	cat
lamb	sheep
owlet	owl
piglet	pig
puppy	dog

QUIZ 34

1. c
2. b
3. b
4. a
5. c

QUIZ 35

1. c
2. a
3. d
4. c
5. a

QUIZ 36

The Acropolis	Greece
Eiffel Tower	France
The Great Wall	China
The Leaning Tower of Pisa	Italy
Machu Picchu	Peru
The Sphinx	Egypt
St Basil's Cathedral	Russia
Statue of Liberty	United States
Stonehenge	United Kingdom
Sydney Opera House	Australia
Taj Mahal	India

Bonjour!

ANSWERS

QUIZ 37

1. d
2. a
3. a
4. b
5. c

QUIZ 38

1. b
2. c
3. a
4. d
5. d

QUIZ 39

1. c
2. d
3. b
4. a

A is Mercury, B is Venus, C is Earth and D is Mars

QUIZ 40

1. b
2. c
3. a
4. a
5. d

QUIZ 41

Arabic	Egypt
English	Australia
French	Switzerland
German	Austria
Hindi	India
Mandarin Chinese	Singapore
Portuguese	Brazil
Russian	Belarus
Spanish	Mexico

QUIZ 42

1. a
2. a
3. c
4. c
5. d

QUIZ 43

Beijing	China
Berlin	Germany
Brussels	Belgium
Cairo	Egypt
Canberra	Australia
London	United Kingdom
Ottawa	Canada
Paris	France
Rome	Italy
Tokyo	Japan
Vienna	Austria
Washington, DC	United States of America

QUIZ 44

1. c
2. b
3. d
4. c
5. c

QUIZ 45

American	United States
British	United Kingdom
Danish	Denmark
Dutch	Netherlands
Finnish	Finland
Greek	Greece
Irish	Ireland
Peruvian	Peru
Spanish	Spain
Swiss	Switzerland
Thai	Thailand

QUIZ 46

1. b
2. a
3. c
4. a
5. d

Blah blah blah!

ANSWERS

QUIZ 47

1. d
2. b
3. a
4. c
5. d

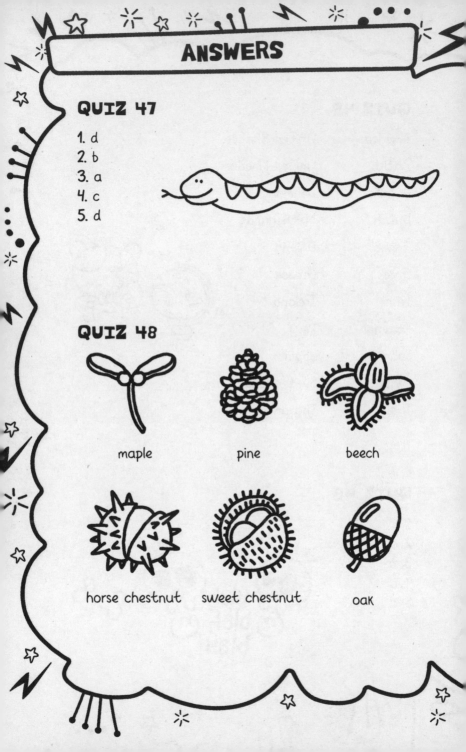

QUIZ 48

maple

pine

beech

horse chestnut

sweet chestnut

oak

QUIZ 49

1. b
2. a
3. d
4. b
5. c

QUIZ 50

bald eagle	United States
bear	Russia
bull	Spain
Koi carp	Japan
Bengal tiger	India
giant panda	China
golden eagle	Mexico
Kangaroo	Australia
Kiwi	New Zealand
lion	Kenya

ANSWERS

QUIZ 51

1. a
2. c
3. d
4. a
5. c

QUIZ 52

Africa: Ethiopia and Morocco

Asia: China and India

Europe: France and the United Kingdom

North America: Canada and the United States

Oceania: Australia and New Zealand

South America: Argentina and Brazil

QUIZ 53

1. d
2. c
3. a
4. b
5. a

QUIZ 54

acre	area
calorie	energy
Celsius and Fahrenheit	temperature
decibel	sound level
gram and stone	weight
knot	wind speed
kilometre and mile	distance
pascal and bar	pressure
second	time
watt	power

ANSWERS

QUIZ 55

1. d
2. d
3. a
4. a
5. a

QUIZ 56

Big countries:
Australia, Canada, China, Russia, United States

Small countries:
Belgium, Israel, Jamaica, Luxembourg, Singapore

QUIZ 57

1. c
2. c
3. b
4. b
5. c

QUIZ 58

1. c
2. b
3. c
4. b
5. d

QUIZ 59

1. c
2. c
3. b
4. c
5. d

QUIZ 60

1. d
2. a
3. c
4. b
5. a

QUIZ 61

1. b
2. d
3. a
4. b
5. b

ANSWERS

QUIZ 62

1. c
2. a
3. a
4. d
5. c

QUIZ 63

1. c
2. b
3. a
4. a
5. b

QUIZ 64

1. a
2. c
3. d
4. c
5. c

QUIZ 65

1. b
2. b
3. a
4. c
5. b

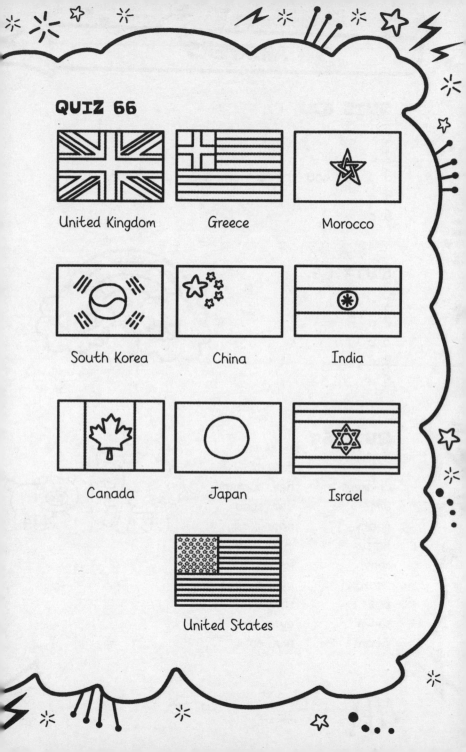

QUIZ 66

United Kingdom

Greece

Morocco

South Korea

China

India

Canada

Japan

Israel

United States

ANSWERS

QUIZ 67

1. b
2. c
3. a, just you. The rest are all going the other way.
4. c
5. c

QUIZ 68

1. c
2. a
3. d
4. c
5. c

QUIZ 69

cattle	cow, bull
chickens	hen, cockerel
deer	doe, stag
goats	nanny, billy
horses	mare, stallion
lions	lioness, lion
peafowl	peahen, peacock
pigs	sow, boar
sheep	ewe, ram
swans	pen, cob

QUIZ 70

1. b
2. d
3. b
4. c
5. c

QUIZ 71

1. a
2. b
3. d
4. c
5. c, it is usually said there are between 48 and 50 countries, but it depends on exactly how you count.

QUIZ 72

1. a
2. b
3. c
4. c
5. a

QUIZ 73

1. b
2. d
3. c
4. c
5. c

QUIZ 74

chimpanzee	50 years
elephant	70 years
fruit fly	25 days
guinea pig	5 years
honeybee	150 days
horse	25 years
male mosquito	10 days (females live up to 50 days)
sea turtle	100 years
wolf	10 years

QUIZ 75

1. c
2. c
3. c
4. a
5. c

QUIZ 76

1. c
2. c
3. b
4. c
5. b

QUIZ 77

1. c
2. a
3. c
4. c
5. a

ANSWERS

QUIZ 78

1. c
2. c
3. a
4. c
5. b

QUIZ 79

1. a
2. c
3. b
4. d
5. a

QUIZ 80

1. a
2. b
3. c
4. d
5. b

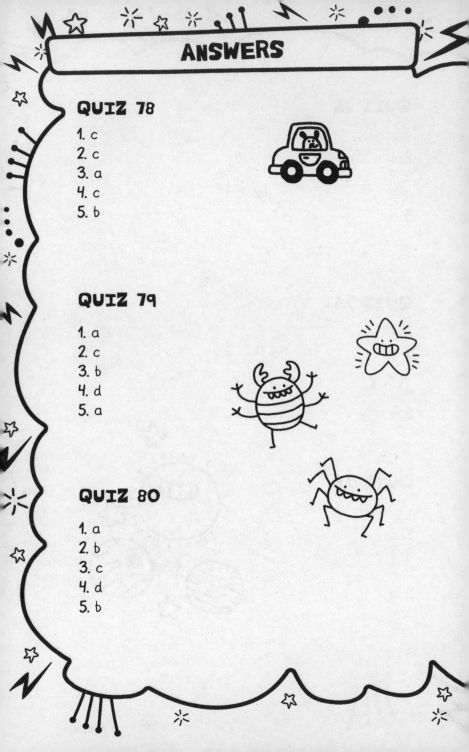

QUIZ 81

In order of increasing size, from smallest to largest, the prefixes are:

Smallest

milli

centi

kilo

mega

giga

tera

Largest

QUIZ 82

1. b
2. a
3. c
4. a
5. b

QUIZ 83

1. a
2. d
3. c
4. a
5. b

ANSWERS

QUIZ 84

1. a
2. d
3. b
4. b
5. c, it was inspired by the Austrian kipfel, which the French turned into a croissant by making it with puff pastry.

QUIZ 85

bonanza: a sudden increase of good luck
catamaran: a boat with two connected hulls
concoction: a mix of various different ingredients
euphoric: feeling really happy
isosceles: a triangle with two sides of equal length
jamboree: a large celebration
kumquat: a fruit that's a bit like a tiny orange
reverie: a daydream, or being lost in thought
sophistry: the use of clever but false arguments
zany: quirky or different in an amusing way

QUIZ 86

1. c
2. d
3. b
4. c
5. a

QUIZ 87

1. c
2. c
3. c
4. a
5. a

QUIZ 88

1. b
2. d
3. b
4. b
5. b

QUIZ 89

1. c, although it is called the pencil 'lead'!
2. c
3. c
4. d
5. b

ANSWERS

QUIZ 90

1. b
2. d
3. b
4. c
5. a

QUIZ 91

In order of increasing population size, from smallest to largest, the countries are:

Ireland (almost 5 million)

Australia (about 25 million)

United Kingdom (almost 67 million)

Japan (almost 127 million)

United States (about 328.5 million)

China (about 1.4 billion)

QUIZ 92

1. b
2. a
3. c
4. c
5. d

QUIZ 93

Ada Lovelace: computer program

Alessandro Volta: battery

Guglielmo Marconi: radio communication

Hedy Lamarr: frequency hopping (used in Wi-Fi and GPS)

Johannes Gutenberg: printing press

Josephine Cochrane: dishwasher

Stephanie Kwolek: Kevlar

Thomas Edison: lightbulb

Tim Berners-Lee: World Wide Web

Yvonne C. Brill: satellite propulsion system

A PLACE FOR YOUR NOTES

NOTES

NOTES

NOTES

NOTES

NOTES

NOTES

NOTES

NOTES

NOTES

NOTES

NOTES

ALSO AVAILABLE: